. . . A book I have made for your dear sake, O soldiers,

And for you, O soul of man, and you, love of comrades . . .

. . . A book separate, not link'd with the rest, nor felt by the intellect;

But you will feel every word. . . .

— Walt Whitman

WALT WHITMAN

Words for America

By

BARBARA KERLEY

Illustrated by BRIAN SELZNICK

Scholastic Press {New York}

WALT WHITMAN

Words for America

◆

By

BARBARA KERLEY

Illustrated by BRIAN SELZNICK

Scholastic Press {New York}

WALT
WHITMAN
LOVED WORDS.

At age 12, he began work as a printer's apprentice, learning to typeset newspaper articles. He saw the boxes of letters as a great mystery, waiting to unfold. Awkwardly, he held the compositor's stick, eager to see the words form — letter by letter — beneath his inky fingers.

Within two years, he was setting articles that he himself had written. After the newspaper was printed, his heart thumped "double-beat" as he smoothed it open and admired his work.

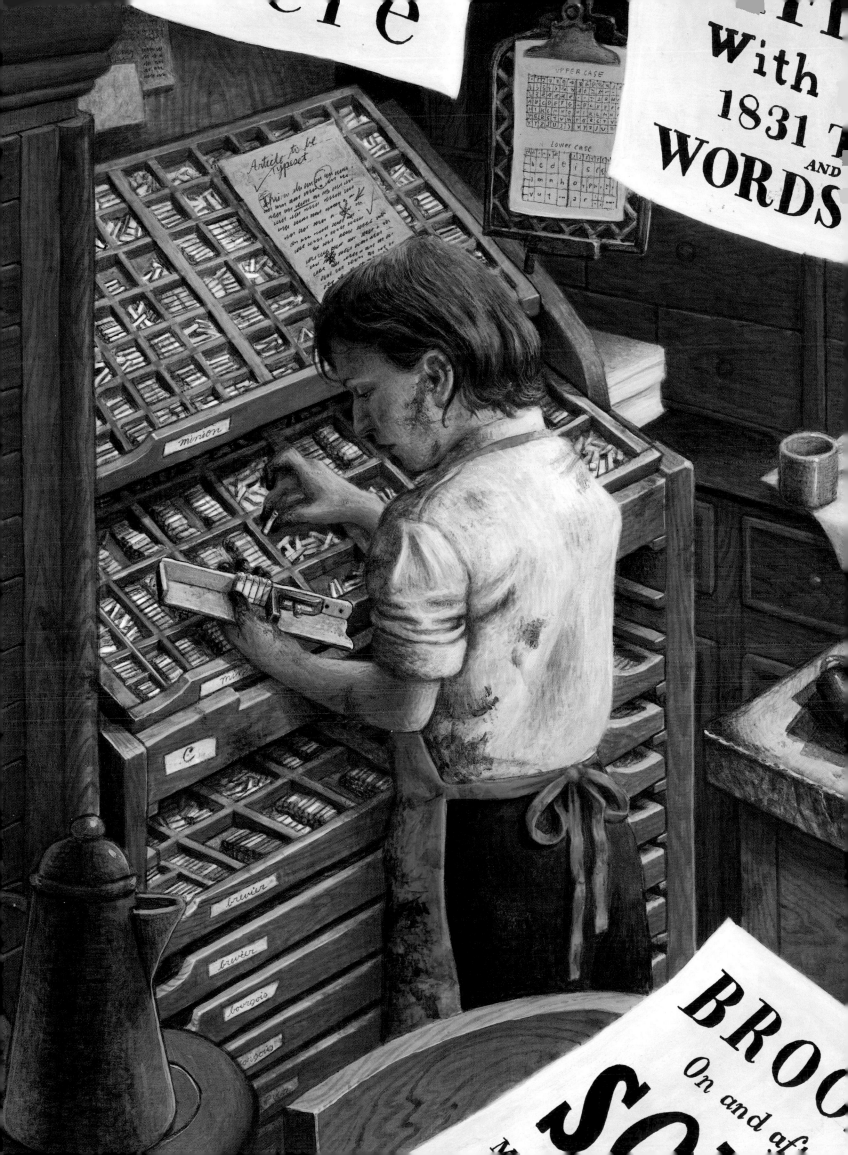

Even when he wasn't working, Walt surrounded himself with words.

He listened to famous speakers and joined a debating society. He attended plays, appreciating a fine performance "in every . . . cell" of his heart and head. At the library, he reveled in the hot sands and fierce genies of *Arabian Nights*, the brave deeds of *Ivanhoe*.

By the time he was nineteen, Walt was writing and printing his own newspaper, the *Long Islander*. He filled the pages with local news, everything from politics to pumpkins to the birth of a three-legged cow. His assistant was his eight-year-old brother, George. Together they delivered the paper with the help of their trusty mare, Nina.

Walt's passion for language was matched only by his passion for rambling. As often as he could, he took the ferry from his home in Brooklyn to the busy streets of Manhattan. There, he saw celebrities and millionaires.

But Walt was just as fascinated by mothers holding babies and carpenters with tools. Shopkeepers, stage-coach drivers, policemen on patrol — in these ordinary Americans he saw the true spirit of the nation.

The countryside beckoned as well. Walt rambled Long Island's quiet roads, past apple orchards and walnut groves. He hiked forests full of hidden springs. In every leaf and blade of grass, he felt America's grace and vigor.

Walt's love affair with language grew even stronger as he explored poetry, for there he found the music of words. Sometimes he'd find a deserted beach, strip down to swim, and then run along the shore, shouting Shakespeare to seagulls and ocean spray.

Slowly, he began writing poems of his own. He made tiny notebooks — a few sheets of paper secured with a ribbon or pin — and carried one in his pocket at all times, so that at a moment's notice he could record what he saw and felt. The notebooks were fertile ground for the seeds of his poems.

In addition to his work as a printer and a writer, Walt had also worked as an office boy, a teacher, and a carpenter. "The genius of the United States," he felt, was in "the common people," and he wanted his poems to reflect their lives.

Unlike the popular poetry of the day, which was carefully metered and rhymed, Walt wrote poems as free-ranging as his big, robust country.

More than anything, he hoped to become the voice of America.

Everywhere he went, Walt scribbled in his notebooks: riding the rails as his train chugged south and west through Maryland, jerking and swaying as his stagecoach jounced over the Allegheny Mountains, steaming slowly down the Mississippi River, past Southern plantations — immense mansions with acres of slaves hoeing cotton, their tumbledown slave quarters huddled nearby.

Walt traveled from New York to New Orleans and home again. He saw America from top to bottom, but his trip left him worried. He feared that the issue of slavery would divide the nation he loved so well. Walt yearned for a new kind of leader: an honest, homespun president who could keep America strong.

And he wondered, was there anything he himself could do to help his country?

Stop this day and

day and shall

and you

origin all

of poems

night with me possess the

Walt responded with words. For the next seven years he worked on his poems celebrating America and her people. He read the poems aloud, shaping their rhythm until he heard in them the roll of ocean waves. Finally, in 1855, with great care and pride, Walt typeset the pages of *Leaves of Grass* — his book for all Americans.

I am of old and young, of the foolish as much
    as the wise . . .
Stuff'd with the stuff that is coarse and stuff'd
    with the stuff that is fine,
One of the Nation of many nations, the smallest
    the same and the largest the same,
A Southerner soon as a Northerner . . .
    . . . a Hoosier, Badger, Buckeye . . .
At home on the hills of Vermont or in the
    woods of Maine, or the Texan ranch . . .
Of every hue and caste am I, of every rank and
    religion. . . .

I resist any thing better than my own diversity,
Breathe the air but leave plenty after me. . . .

Walt's new style of poetry struck some readers with its freshness and vigor. Others, however, thought the poems clumsy and crude.

Walt wrote on, revising the poems and adding many new ones. He tried not to get discouraged. He believed in his poems, no matter what the critics said. But he was disappointed to find that his poems weren't reaching the "common people."

How could he speak for all Americans if they did not read his book?

All the while, Walt was living with his mother and brothers. At the breakfast table, Walt and George shared a pot of coffee as they read the morning papers and discussed the news of the day.

The news was troubling. By the spring of 1861, tensions between the North and South had risen. Seven Southern states had already seceded from the Union, convinced that the newly elected president, Abraham Lincoln, planned to end slavery — something the South would not tolerate.

A few weeks later, Walt joined thirty thousand New Yorkers hoping to catch a glimpse of Lincoln on his way to Washington, D.C., for his inauguration.

Watching Lincoln step from his carriage, Walt wrote in his notebook: ". . . the stovepipe hat push'd back on the head, the dark-brown complexion, the seam'd and wrinkled yet canny-looking face . . . the hands held behind as he stood observing the people. All was comparative and ominous silence. . . ."

Walt wasn't sure quite what to make of Lincoln. Like many in the crowd, he was more concerned that Lincoln's inauguration might lead the country — divided by the issue of slavery — straight into war.

Barely a month into Lincoln's presidency, Southern forces fired upon Fort Sumter, a Union garrison in Charleston harbor, South Carolina.

The Civil War had started.

THE CIV

18

CIVIL WAR

61

WALT

was too old to fight, but he proudly watched as his brother George, in his blue Union jacket, marched off to war.

Union forces, however, were soundly beaten during the first major conflict, the Battle of Bull Run. Walt felt full of "gloom and apprehension." He wrote poems for the newspapers to rally people behind the Union cause, to reunite the country.

Beat! beat! drums!—blow! bugles! blow!
Through the windows—through doors—burst
 like a ruthless force. . . .

Still, with a growing sense of dread, Walt read the letters George wrote home, of bullets flying overhead and comrades shot and killed.

When Walt went to the Broadway Hospital in Manhattan to visit an injured stagecoach driver, he saw haunting reminders of the war: soldiers brought up from the battlefront. He wrote in a newspaper article, "I have many hours afterwards, in far different scenes, had the pale faces, the look of death, the appealing eyes, come curiously of a sudden, plainly before me."

He began spending time with these soldiers, hoping to cheer them, wishing he could do more.

Every morning as he drank his coffee, Walt scanned the newspapers, checking the lists of wounded and dead, worrying about George. He pored over hundreds of names:

John Clare, 69th New-York – hip.
D.C. Grindle, Co. K, 16th Maine – leg.
F. Hanscom, Co. D, 2d Delaware – eye.
Major Harghan, 88th N.Y., killed.

On the morning of December 16, 1862, Walt read George's name.

There was no information about George's injury. Was he badly hurt?

Walt rushed toward Washington and spent the next two days and nights searching the hospitals. He was tired, hungry, and very discouraged. He couldn't find George anywhere.

Grimly, Walt caught an army train headed south, reaching the camp hospitals in Falmouth, Virginia, the next day. There, men lay in rough tents pitched on the frozen ground. They slept on layers of twigs covered by blankets. Walt hurried from tent to tent, from man to broken man, feeling huge and helpless.

At last, he found his brother.

George's cheek had been pierced by an exploding shell. Luckily, the wound wasn't serious.

Walt later wrote home to their mother, ". . . When I found dear brother George, and found that he was alive and well, O you may imagine how trifling all my little cares and difficulties seemed — they vanished into nothing."

Walt stayed at camp for over a week, visiting the hospitals. He wrote in his notebook: ". . . I go around from one case to another. I do not see that I do much good, but I cannot leave them."

At night, Walt slept in George's tent. He loved learning the soldiers' lingo — "bivouac" for camp; "army pies and wash" for crackers and coffee.

Sitting around the campfires, he met men from all over the North and heard their tales of battle. As Walt learned more about their struggles and experienced their "hard accommodations" for himself, he began to give these soldiers a voice.

By the bivouac's fitful flame,
A procession winding around me, solemn
    and sweet and slow—but first I note . . .
The darkness lit by spots of kindled fire,
    the silence . . .
While wind in procession thoughts,
    O tender and wondrous thoughts,
Of life and death, of home and the past
    and loved, and of those that are far away. . . .

By now, George's cheek had healed. It was time for Walt to go. He offered to help transfer the wounded to the hospitals in Washington. Then the two brothers said good-bye.

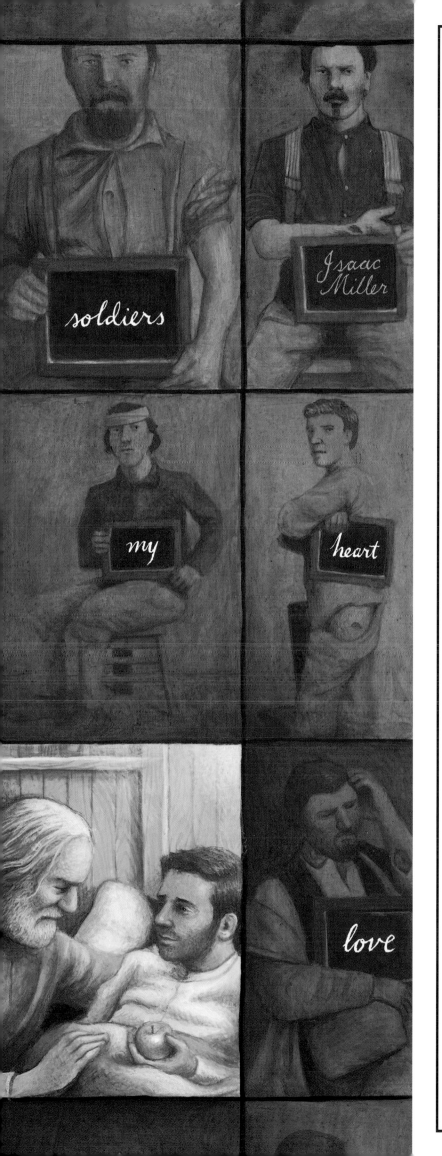

soldiers

Isaac Miller

my

heart

love

In Washington, Walt was appalled by the suffering the soldiers endured: gunshot wounds, typhoid fever, amputations. Soon, each face had a name.

Walt intended to stay only a few weeks. But when he saw that his good cheer helped some patients even more than medicine, he knew he could not leave, writing home, ". . . many of them have come to depend on seeing me, and having me sit by them a few minutes, as if for their lives."

Walt picked up a small job, a few hours a day in a government office. The pay wasn't much, but it was enough, with donations from friends, to fill a sack with "little gifts."

David S. Giles – Company F 28th New Jersey Volunteers – wants an apple
Janus Mafield – 7th Virginia Volunteers – 2 oranges
Henry D. Boardman – Company B 27th Connecticut Volunteers – wants a rice pudding, not very sweet

Walt jotted it all down in his tiny notebooks as he made his hospital rounds.

Black, white, Union, Confederate — Walt nursed whomever he saw. He fed men too weak to eat. He bathed fevered foreheads with cool, wet cloths. Sometimes he changed the dressings on a man's wounds.

. . . Bearing the bandages, water and sponge,
Straight and swift to my wounded I go . . .
To each and all one after another I draw near, not one do I miss . . .

Winter turned to spring, and spring turned to summer. Walt mourned the passing of so many young lives.

At times he had to busy himself, bustling around the hospital to avoid crying. "... To see such things & not be able to help them is awful," he wrote home. "I feel almost ashamed of being so well & whole. ..."

After leaving the hospital he'd find himself trembling at what he had seen. Then he'd walk for hours through the dark streets under the still, silent moon.

In the mornings, as he headed to his job, Walt often saw President Abraham Lincoln ride by. The two bowed to each other, the war weighing on them both. Walt felt Lincoln's determination to heal the country. He began to see Lincoln as a captain, guiding his ship through troubled waters, and wrote in his notebook: "his face & manner . . . are inexpressibly sweet. . . . I love the President personally."

Walt continued writing his poems and hoped for a swift end to the fighting.

But the war dragged on through its third year, and more and more men arrived at the hospitals every day.

As Walt spent time with them, he came to understand America more deeply. Despite their suffering and sadness, the soldiers were courageous, dedicated, even hopeful. Walt found in them, he wrote to a friend, ". . . the best expression of American character I have ever seen. . . ."

And he knew that his poems celebrating Americans would not be complete until he honored these soldiers.

Walt grew so attached to them that he sometimes stayed at the hospital late into the evening, keeping close but quiet company so that a young soldier would not have to die alone.

Washington   August 10   1863

Mr and Mrs Haskell,

   . . . I thought it would be soothing to you to have a few lines about the last days of your son Erastus. . . . Many nights I sat in the hospital by his bedside till far in the night — The lights would be put out — yet I would sit there silently, hours, late, perhaps fanning him — he always liked to have me sit there, but never cared to talk — I shall never forget those nights. . . .

   I write to you this letter, because I would do something at least in his memory. . . . He is one of the thousands of our unknown American young men in the ranks about whom there is no record or fame, no fuss made about their dying so unknown, but I find in them the real precious & royal ones of this land. . . .

   Mr and Mrs Haskell . . . though we are strangers & shall probably never see each other, I send you . . . my love —

Walt Whitman

Day after day, Walt returned to the hospitals, trying to stay cheerful. But by the end of June 1864, he was exhausted. When the doctors ordered him to take a break, Walt was too tired to protest. He traveled home to rest at his mother's house and work on his book of Civil War poetry. He called the book *Drum-Taps*, a sound that always stirred him when he heard soldiers marching.

Walt wrote to a friend that he would "move heaven and earth" to publish the book as soon as he was able.

By January Walt felt stronger. He returned to Washington, caring for the soldiers as often as his health

allowed. But he was home visiting his family on April 9, 1865, when the South surrendered to the North.

After four long years, at last the Civil War was over!

Walt and his family barely had time to rejoice. Five days after the war ended, tragedy stunned the nation: Abraham Lincoln was assassinated.

Walt was too upset to eat or even speak. He read the newspapers' grim accounts. Then he walked the streets of Manhattan, rain dripping from the black banners of mourning.

A few days later, Walt boarded a train for Washington. Heartsick, he spent the next several months composing poems that voiced America's grief.

O Captain! my Captain! our fearful trip is done,
The ship has weather'd every rack, the prize we
sought is won,
The port is near, the bells I hear, the people all
exulting,
While follow eyes the steady keel, the vessel grim
and daring;
But O heart! heart! heart!
O the bleeding drops of red,
Where on the deck my Captain lies,
Fallen cold and dead. . . .

Walt's words helped him say good-bye to Lincoln, as well as to the war. Now Walt, like the rest of the country, turned toward peace.

Slowly, America began to heal, led by her new president, Andrew Johnson. As the last wartime soldiers recovered, Walt continued his hospital visits, with growing certainty that his small part in helping his country had been "the greatest privilege and satisfaction" of his life.

And soon, he finished his book of Civil War poetry, *Drum-Taps*. News of the poems spread after a friend published a tribute to Walt and wrote letters to newspapers about Walt's years of hospital service.

As people learned of the sacrifices made by "The Good Gray Poet," they read his poetry.

. . . For all my days—not those of peace alone—
    the days of war the same . . .
For all the brave strong men—devoted, hardy
    men—who've forward sprung in freedom's
    help, all years, all lands . . .
Thanks—joyful thanks!—a soldier's, traveler's
    thanks.

And as they read, they heard — in every line — the voice of the nation.

Whoever you are
now
that you be
my

I place my hand upon you

poem

AUTHOR'S NOTE

In January 2001, I was just sitting down to begin work on a new book when I received a surprise in the mail. Brian Selznick, who had illustrated our book *The Dinosaurs of Waterhouse Hawkins*, had sent me a little gift: a beautiful medallion of Walt Whitman, a butterfly perched on his finger. Brian had made the medallion to commemorate an uncle who liked butterflies. I was moved by the expression on Walt's face: thoughtful, joyful, alive.

I'd loved Walt's poems for years, and always had it in the back of my mind that one day I'd write a book about him. As soon as I saw the medallion, I set the other project aside.

In researching Walt's life, his Civil War experience quickly captured me. I knew I wanted it to be the focus of my book on this most remarkable man.

WALT

Walt Whitman was born on May 31, 1819, the son of a carpenter and a homemaker. His father built houses — and moved the family — all over Long Island and Brooklyn, New York, both places the inspiration for many of Walt's poems.

The family had eight children: Jesse, Walt, Mary, and Hannah, then three boys named after U.S. presidents — Andrew Jackson, George Washington, and Thomas Jefferson — and, finally, Edward. Walt remained very close to his family — and especially to his mother — his whole life.

Walt left school at age eleven to begin work as an office boy. His first employer gave him a library card, which Walt later called "the signal event of my life up to that time." Through reading and his later work as a printer's apprentice, Walt learned to appreciate the written word. All his life he continued to educate himself by reading literature, history, and philosophy.

The onset of the Civil War deeply upset Walt. At age forty-one, he was too old to enlist, but even if he had been younger, it's difficult to imagine Walt as a soldier, firing a weapon. He felt a special connection with people — friends *and* strangers — considering them all comrades.

Like many Northerners of the time, including Abraham Lincoln, Walt recognized the evils of slavery but viewed splitting the country in two as worse. Though not an abolitionist himself, Walt wrote compassionately of the plight of slaves in *Leaves of Grass*.

. . . Within there runs blood,
The same old blood! the same red-running blood!
There swells and jets a heart, there all passions, desires,
reachings, aspirations,
(Do you think they are not there because they are not express'd
in parlors and lecture-rooms?) . . . .

How do you know who shall come from the offspring of his
offspring through the centuries?
(Who might you find you have come from yourself, if you
could trace back through the centuries?) . . .

And during the course of the war, Walt visited hospitals where black soldiers were treated, bringing his care and comfort to them as well.

Easing the suffering of soldiers was Walt's way of attempting to heal the country, but it took a heavy toll. Daily exposure to the soldiers' illnesses and the profound emotional strain permanently affected Walt's good health. Near the end of the war he suffered from dizziness, weakness, and fainting spells. For the rest of his life he never regained the physical vigor he had enjoyed before the war.

LINCOLN

Although most Americans now consider Abraham Lincoln to be one of our country's greatest presidents, he was not a popular choice when he was first elected. Like many Americans, Walt grew to love Lincoln during his presidency, later calling him "the sweetest, wisest soul of all my days and lands."

The two probably never spoke, but Walt often saw Lincoln on the streets of Washington, and even inside the White House when he joined the crowds of well-wishers after Lincoln's second inauguration.

Walt probably didn't know that Lincoln had been an admirer of his poetry for years. When *Leaves of Grass* was first published in 1855, Lincoln's law partner brought a copy into their office in Springfield, Illinois, and Lincoln liked the poetry so much that he took the book home with him. However, some of the book's poems about the human body shocked the Lincoln household. The next day, Lincoln brought the book back, reporting that he "had barely saved it from being purified by fire by the women." After that, the book stayed at the office, and Lincoln often picked it up and read the poems out loud.

Two of Walt's poems commemorating Lincoln, "O Captain! My Captain!" and "When Lilacs Last in the Dooryard Bloom'd," remain among his most popular today.

AFTER THE WAR

In January 1873, Walt suffered a stroke, leaving him paralyzed on his left side. He moved from Washington, D.C., into his brother George's home in Camden, New Jersey. Although Walt's health continued to plague him, he still traveled, saw old friends, and made many new ones. He wrote poems, and in 1875 published *Memoranda During the War*, his account — taken from his notebooks — of his Civil War experience.

George later moved to Burlington, New Jersey, but Walt, wanting to stay near his friends in Camden, bought himself a little house on Mickle Street. He hired a housekeeper — with a cat, dog, parrot, and canary — to cook and clean for him.

In 1892, nearly twenty-seven years after the war's end, Walt died at age seventy-two, surrounded by friends. For three hours on the day of his funeral, a line of mourners sometimes three blocks long came to pay their respects. Alongside literary figures stood shopkeepers, tradesmen, and schoolchildren.

. . . The last scud of day holds back for me,
It flings my likeness after the rest and true as any on the
shadow'd wilds,
It coaxes me to the vapor and the dusk. . . .

You will hardly know who I am or what I mean,
But I shall be good health to you nevertheless,
And filter and fibre your blood.

Failing to fetch me at first keep encouraged,
Missing me one place search another,
I stop somewhere waiting for you.

ILLUSTRATOR'S NOTE

This photo of Walt inspired this book. I found the picture on the Internet when I was researching butterflies to make the medallion that Barbara mentions in her author's note. Little did I know that it would lead us to the Civil War and

Abraham Lincoln and the incredible life of one of America's greatest poets.

After I read an early draft of Barbara's manuscript, my adventures began. On Long Island, I visited Walt's birth home at West Hills in Huntington Station, as well as Old Bethpage Village Restoration, a reconstructed nineteenth-century town with an actual house where Walt might have stayed at one time. I saw the photos of Walt held by the Brooklyn Public Library, and I spent time in the Rare Book Room of the New York Public Library, where I held in my hand one of Walt's original handmade notebooks. I turned the pages of this notebook and saw how he had tied the thread that held it together, and I read the entries that he had written lightly in pencil. It was thrilling. I visited the Museum of Printing History in Houston, Texas. At Bowne and Co. Stationers, part of the South Street Seaport Museum in Manhattan, I was given a special typesetting demonstration at a working nineteenth-century printing press by the master printer Barbara Henry. When I was nearly done with the book, I traveled to Camden, New Jersey. There I visited the house where Walt lived for the last eight years of his life. I saw an actual pair of his shoes and stood beside the bed where he died. I then took a short cab ride to his grave (pictured on the back endpapers), a few miles away, where I found little gifts had been left for him — two oranges and a paper crane.

My experiences researching Walt's life found their way into this book, from the trays of type that Walt is using as a boy (Ms. Henry told me that the capital letters were placed on the upper shelf, and the others on the lower shelf, which is why we now have the terms "uppercase" and "lowercase"!) to the big green genie that is loosely based on illustrations from copies of *Arabian Nights* that Walt could have seen as a boy. All of my illustrated daguerreotypes of soldiers — those going off to war and those injured by the war — are based on actual photographs of the young men. When first sketching out my ideas for the pictures in this book, I had imagined a spread with rows and rows of young soldiers at the beginning of the Civil War, and later, while doing my research, I found an indispensable book called *The Civil War* by Geoffrey C. Ward, Ric Burns, and Ken Burns. In it, I discovered a spread of actual photographs of young soldiers arranged in rows just like the picture I had imagined. I used it as reference for my book. A later spread in *The Civil War* showed photographs of injured soldiers, and that inspired me as well. The chalkboards that the injured soldiers are holding were actually used in some photos for identification purposes. In the picture where Walt and George are reunited in the field hospital, what can't be seen are the holes the soldiers had dug beneath those rough tents, which some of the wounded crawled into, trying to keep warm.

I also read several biographies on Walt, but most

importantly, in my quest to try to understand him, I read *Leaves of Grass*, both the very short 1855 edition as well as the much expanded final edition of 1892, called the deathbed edition. Reading Walt's poetry is a very immediate experience. Over and over again we are reminded that Walt himself is here with us, experiencing what we experience, seeing what we see, feeling what we feel. As Walt says in the poem "Crossing Brooklyn Ferry," "It avails not, time nor place—distance avails not, / I am with you, you men and women of a generation, or ever so many generations hence . . ." That idea was very important for me while I worked on this book.

There was one other statement Walt made that haunted me, and it comes from a poem also in *Leaves of Grass*, called "So Long." It says, "Camerado, this is no book, / Who touches this touches a man." I hope you will feel the same way about the book you are now holding in your hands.

A NOTE ON THE POEMS

Editions of Walt Whitman's poetry vary widely. They reflect Walt's love of revision and his occasional use of non-standard punctuation, as well as the different choices that editors of various editions of his poetry have made. We have chosen to excerpt the poems in *Walt Whitman: Words for America* from the Norton Critical Edition of *Leaves of Grass* (1973). This authoritative text of Walt's final edition in 1892 employs standardized punctuation, allowing readers of our book to identify when the text of a poem has been shortened and replaced by ellipses.

It was important to us to include here as much of Walt's poetry as possible. However, most of his poems are simply too long to reprint in full. The text below and the pages that follow provide longer excerpts of the poems we have cited and, whenever possible, the entire poem as written.

POEMS
Section 16 of "Song of Myself,"
Leaves of Grass

I am of old and young, of the foolish as much as the wise,
Regardless of others, ever regardful of others,
Maternal as well as paternal, a child as well as a man,
Stuff'd with the stuff that is coarse and stuff'd with the
　　stuff that is fine,
One of the Nation of many nations, the smallest the same
　　and the largest the same,
A Southerner soon as a Northerner, a planter nonchalant

and hospitable down by the Oconee I live,
A Yankee bound my own way ready for trade, my joints the
　　limberest joints on earth and the sternest joints on
　　earth,
A Kentuckian walking the vale of the Elkhorn in my
　　deer-skin leggings, a Louisianian or Georgian,
A boatman over lakes or bays or along coasts, a Hoosier,
　　Badger, Buckeye;
At home on Kanadian snow-shoes or up in the bush, or
　　with fishermen off Newfoundland,
At home in the fleet of ice-boats, sailing with the rest and
　　tacking,
At home on the hills of Vermont or in the woods of Maine,
　　or the Texan ranch,
Comrade of Californians, comrade of free North-
　　Westerners, (loving their big proportions,)
Comrade of raftsmen and coalmen, comrade of all who
　　shake hands and welcome to drink and meat,
A learner with the simplest, a teacher of the thought-
　　fullest,
A novice beginning yet experient of myriads of seasons,
Of every hue and caste am I, of every rank and religion,
A farmer, mechanic, artist, gentleman, sailor, quaker,
Prisoner, fancy-man, rowdy, lawyer, physician, priest.

I resist any thing better than my own diversity,
Breathe the air but leave plenty after me,
And am not stuck up, and am in my place.

(The moth and the fish-eggs are in their place,
The bright suns I see and the dark suns I cannot see are in
　　their place,
The palpable is in its place and the impalpable is in its
　　place.)

"Beat! Beat! Drums!" (complete),
Leaves of Grass

Beat! beat! drums!—blow! bugles! blow!
Through the windows—through doors—burst like a
　　ruthless force,
Into the solemn church, and scatter the congregation,
Into the school where the scholar is studying;
Leave not the bridegroom quiet—no happiness must he
　　have now with his bride,

Nor the peaceful farmer any peace, ploughing his field or
  gathering his grain,
So fierce you whirr and pound you drums—so shrill you
  bugles blow.

Beat! beat! drums—blow! bugles! blow!
Over the traffic of cities—over the rumble of wheels in the
  streets;
Are beds prepared for sleepers at night in the houses? no
  sleepers must sleep in those beds,
No bargainers' bargains by day—no brokers or
  speculators—would they continue?
Would the talkers be talking? would the singer attempt to
  sing?
Would the lawyer rise in the court to state his case before
  the judge?
Then rattle quicker, heavier drums—you bugles wilder
  blow.

Beat! beat! drums!—blow! bugles! blow!
Make no parley—stop for no expostulation,
Mind not the timid—mind not the weeper or prayer,
Mind not the old man beseeching the young man,
Let not the child's voice be heard, nor the mother's
  entreaties,
Make even the trestles to shake the dead where they lie
  awaiting the hearses,
So strong you thump O terrible drums—so loud you bugles
  blow.

"By the Bivouac's Fitful Flame" (complete),
Leaves of Grass

By the bivouac's fitful flame,
A procession winding around me, solemn and sweet and
  slow—but first I note,
The tents of the sleeping army, the fields' and woods' dim
  outline,
The darkness lit by spots of kindled fire, the silence,
Like a phantom far or near an occasional figure moving,
The shrubs and trees, (as I lift my eyes they seem to be
  stealthily watching me,)
While wind in procession thoughts, O tender and wondrous
  thoughts,
Of life and death, of home and the past and loved, and of

those that are far away;
A solemn and slow procession there as I sit on the ground,
By the bivouac's fitful flame.

from "The Wound Dresser,"
Leaves of Grass

. . . Bearing the bandages, water and sponge,
Straight and swift to my wounded I go,
Where they lie on the ground after the battle brought in,
Where their priceless blood reddens the grass the ground,
Or to the rows of the hospital tent, or under the roof'd
  hospital,
To the long rows of cots up and down each side I return,
To each and all one after another I draw near, not one do I
  miss . . .

"O Captain! My Captain!" (complete),
Leaves of Grass

O Captain! my Captain! our fearful trip is done,
The ship has weather'd every rack, the prize we sought is
  won,
The port is near, the bells I hear, the people all exulting,
While follow eyes the steady keel, the vessel grim and
  daring;
      But O heart! heart! heart!
          O the bleeding drops of red,
              Where on the deck my Captain lies,
                  Fallen cold and dead.

O Captain! my Captain! rise up and hear the bells;
Rise up—for you the flag is flung—for you the bugle trills,
For you bouquets and ribbon'd wreaths—for you the
  shores a-crowding,
For you they call, the swaying mass, their eager faces
  turning;
      Here Captain! dear father!
          This arm beneath your head!
              It is some dream that on the deck,
                  You've fallen cold and dead.

My Captain does not answer, his lips are pale and still,
My father does not feel my arm, he has no pulse nor will,

The ship is anchor'd safe and sound, its voyage closed and
    done,
From fearful trip the victor ship comes in with object won;
    Exult O shores, and ring O bells!
      But I with mournful tread,
        Walk the deck my Captain lies,
          Fallen cold and dead.

"Thanks in Old Age" (complete),
Leaves of Grass

Thanks in old age—thanks ere I go,
For health, the midday sun, the impalpable air—for life,
    mere life,
For precious ever-lingering memories, (of you my mother
    dear—you, father—you, brothers, sisters, friends,)
For all my days—not those of peace alone—the days of war
    the same,
For gentle words, caresses, gifts from foreign lands,
For shelter, wine and meat—for sweet appreciation,
(You distant, dim unknown—or young or old—countless,
    unspecified, readers belov'd,
We never met, and ne'er shall meet—and yet our souls
    embrace, long, close and long;)
For beings, groups, love, deeds, words, books—for colors,
    forms,
For all the brave strong men—devoted, hardy men—
    who've forward sprung in freedom's help, all years, all
    lands,
For braver, stronger, more devoted men—(a special laurel
    ere I go, to life's war's chosen ones,
The cannoneers of song and thought—the great
    artillerists—the foremost leaders, captains of the
    soul:)
As soldier from an ended war return'd—As traveler out of
    myriads, to the long procession retrospective,
Thanks—joyful thanks!—a soldier's, traveler's thanks.

from Section 7, "I Sing the Body Electric,"
Leaves of Grass

Within there runs blood,
The same old blood! the same red-running blood!

There swells and jets a heart, there all passions, desires,
    reachings, aspirations,
(Do you think they are not there because they are not
    express'd in parlors and lecture-rooms?)

This is not only one man, this the father of those who shall
    be fathers in their turns,
In him the start of populous states and rich republics,
Of him countless immortal lives with countless
    embodiments and enjoyments.

How do you know who shall come from the offspring of his
    offspring through the centuries?
(Who might you find you have come from yourself, if you
    could trace back through the centuries?)

Section 52, "Song of Myself,"
Leaves of Grass

The spotted hawk swoops by and accuses me, he complains
    of my gab and my loitering.

I too am not a bit tamed, I too am untranslatable,
I sound my barbaric yawp over the roofs of the world.

The last scud of day holds back for me,
It flings my likeness after the rest and true as any on the
    shadow'd wilds,
It coaxes me to the vapor and the dusk.

I depart as air, I shake my white locks at the runaway sun,
I effuse my flesh in eddies, and drift it in lacy jags.

I bequeath myself to the dirt to grow from the grass I love,
If you want me again look for me under your boot-soles.

You will hardly know who I am or what I mean,
But I shall be good health to you nevertheless,
And filter and fibre your blood.

Failing to fetch me at first keep encouraged,
Missing me one place search another,
I stop somewhere waiting for you.

SOURCES

QUOTES IN THE BOOK (IN SEQUENTIAL ORDER) COME FROM:

"double-beat." Walt Whitman. *Specimen Days & Collect.* (New York: Dover Publications Inc., 1995), p. 195. Hereafter cited as *Specimen.*

"in every...cell." *Specimen*, p. 19.

"The genius of..." "Preface 1855" to *Leaves of Grass.* Walt Whitman. Sculley Bradley and Harold W. Blodgett, eds. (New York: W. W. Norton & Co., 1973), p. 712. Hereafter cited as *Leaves.*

"the stovepipe hat..." Walt Whitman. *Memoranda During the War.* (Bedford: Applewood Books, 1990), p. 28. Hereafter cited as *Memoranda.*

"gloom and apprehension." *Specimen*, p. 25.

"I have many hours..." Charles Glicksberg. *Walt Whitman and the Civil War.* (New York: A. S. Barnes & Co. Inc., 1963), p. 29. Hereafter cited as Glicksberg.

"John Clare, 69th New-York-hip..." *The New York Times*, December 16, 1862, p. 1.

"When I found..." Edwin Haviland Miller, ed. *Walt Whitman: The Correspondence, Volume I.* (New York: New York University Press, 1961), p. 59. Hereafter cited as *Correspondence.*

"I go around..." *Memoranda*, p. 6.

"hard accommodations." Glicksberg, p. 71.

"many of them..." *Correspondence*, p. 77.

"little gifts." *Memoranda*, p. 7.

"David S. Giles..." Notebook #94, images 14 and 39, Library of Congress. http://lcweb2.loc.gov/learn/collections/ww/history.html.

"To see such things..." *Correspondence*, pp. 99–100.

"his face & manner..." Glicksberg, p. 138.

"the best expression..." *Correspondence*, p. 69.

"Mr and Mrs Haskell..." *Correspondence*, pp. 127–129.

"move heaven and earth." *Correspondence*, pp. 235–236.

"the greatest privilege..." *Memoranda*, p. 73.

"The Good Gray Poet." William Douglas O'Connor. Self-published. Washington, D.C., 1865. See: http://www.iath.virginia.edu/fdw/volume2/price/remembered/good_gray_poet.htm.

QUOTES IN THE ART COME FROM:

"A book I have made..." "Shut Not Your Doors." Walt Whitman. *Drum-taps.* (New York: [s.n.], 1865). p. 8.

"Stop this day..." "Song of Myself." *Leaves*, p. 30.

"O my soldiers..." "Dirge for Two Veterans." *Leaves*, p. 315.

"Whoever you are..." "To You." *Leaves*, p. 233.

"I depart as air..." "Song of Myself." *Leaves*, p. 89.

QUOTES IN THE AUTHOR'S AND ILLUSTRATOR'S NOTES COME FROM:

"the signal event..." *Specimen*, p. 15.

"the sweetest, wisest..." "When Lilacs Last in the Dooryard Bloom'd." *Leaves*, p. 337.

"had barely saved..." Gay Wilson Allen. *The Solitary Singer.* (New York: The Macmillan Company, 1955), pp. 175–76.

"Crossing Brooklyn Ferry." *Leaves*, p. 160.

"So Long!" *Leaves*, p. 505.

Of the additional two dozen sources consulted, the following were especially helpful: *A Whitman Chronology.* Joann P. Krieg. Iowa City: University of Iowa Press, 1998 and *The Better Angel: Walt Whitman in the Civil War.* Roy Morris, Jr. New York: Oxford University Press, 2000.

To learn more about Walt's Civil War years, young readers can read his own account, *Memoranda During the War* (reprinted by Applewood Books, 1990), and visit the Library of Congress's Web site: http://memory.loc.gov/ammem/wwhtml/wwhome.html.

For Gennifer Choldenko and Julie Cowan:
two wise souls
— B. K.

For David Serlin: "Here, take this gift . . ."
— B. S.

THE AUTHOR AND ILLUSTRATOR WISH TO THANK:
Wayne Furman, Office of Special Collections, and the staff of the Rare Books Division, New York Public Library; Jeanne Lamb, Donnell Library Central Children's Room, New York Public Library; the staff of the Picture Collection, New York Public Library; Alice L. Birney, Manuscript Division, Library of Congress, Washington, D.C.; Dick Ryan and Barbara Bart, Walt Whitman Birthplace Association, Huntington Station, New York; James McKenna, Old Bethpage Village Restoration, Old Bethpage, New York; Leo Blake and Richard K. Dyer, Walt Whitman House, Camden, New Jersey; Sarah McNett, Kelly Papinchak, and Gordon Rouze, the Museum of Printing History, Houston, Texas; Barbara Henry, Master Printer, Bowne and Co. Stationers, South Street Seaport Museum, New York, New York; David Robinson, Rare Book and Special Collections, Library of Congress; and, most especially, Chattanooga, Tennessee, historian and Civil War scholar Roy Morris, Jr., author of *The Better Angel: Walt Whitman in the Civil War.*

Text copyright © 2004 by Barbara Kerley Kelly
Illustrations copyright © 2004 by Brian Selznick

LIBRARY OF CONGRESS CATALOGING-IN-PUBLICATION DATA
Kerley, Barbara.
Walt Whitman: Words for America / by Barbara Kerley; illustrated by Brian Selznick.—1st ed.
p. cm.
Summary: A biography of the American poet whose compassion led him to nurse soldiers during the Civil War, to give voice to the nation's grief at Lincoln's assassination, and to capture the true American spirit in verse.
ISBN 0-439-35791-8
1. Whitman, Walt, 1819-1892—Juvenile literature. 2. United States—History—Civil War, 1861-1865—Medical care—Juvenile literature. 3. Poets, American—19th century—Biography—Juvenile literature. 4. Nurses—United States—Biography—Juvenile literature. [1. Whitman, Walt, 1819-1892. 2. United States—History—Civil War, 1861-1865. 3. Poets, American. 4. Nurses.] I. Selznick, Brian, ill. II. Title. PS3232.K47 2004 811'.3—dc22 2003020085

12 11 10 9 8 7 6 5 4 3   04 05 06 07 08
Printed in Singapore 46   First edition, October 2004

Photograph of Walt Whitman © Corbis.
The text type was set in 12-point Scotch Roman, Walt's favorite typeface, which he used in the original edition of *Leaves of Grass*. The book was designed by Brian Selznick and David Saylor.

. . . I depart as air, I shake my white locks at the runaway sun,

I effuse my flesh in eddies and drift it in lacy jags.

I bequeath myself to the dirt to grow from the grass I love.

If you want me again look for me under your bootsoles. . . .

— Walt Whitman